Covid-19 Review

A Guide for Journaling

Yvonne Hampden

A Ymah Rivera Publication

North Carolina

Layout, Design: Jonathan Gullery

Edited by Yvonne Hampden

For information contact:
yhampden@yahoo.com

www.yvonnehampden.com

Divinely Inspired

by our One True Love,

the Lord!

And ye shall be holy unto me:
for I the Lord am holy, and have severed
you from other people,
that ye should be mine.!

Leviticus 20:26

VIRUS:

A Minute Parasitic Microorganism,
may replicate only within a cell
of a living plant or animal host.

More than 200 viruses have been identified
as capable of causing disease in humans.

-Mosby's Pocket Dictionary Of Medicine,
Nursing, & Allied Health, 3Rd Edition

Cherish Today

Who Is God?

Who is God? I'd like to know
Up above, white as the snow

Blue as the sky, round as a ball
Have mercy on me
             And hear my call.

Dark as the night
             bright as the sun
As powerful as life taken by a gun.

Who is God?
             A master or slave
To life's beginning, To death's remains...

cherish Today

Do you know?

God 'First'!

cherish Today

Do you know?

The devil is evil!

But, he is only the

ignorance in Man...

When we know better we can

do better!

Cherish Today

Do you know?

God Bless the USA!

May we all give thanks!

cherish Today

Do you know?

I believe in God the Good!

The One Power
&
Presence in the Universe!

Cherish Today

Do you know?

God loves us & all his

CREATION!

cherish Today

Do you know?

...A Prayer...

Lamb of God, you take away

the Sins of the World!

Have mercy on Us!

cherish Today

Do you know?

I AM...

A CHILD OF GOD!

Cherish Today

Do you know?

I AM...

A WOMAN OF FAITH!

cherish Today

Do you know?

CHRISTIAN, MUSLIM,
JEWISH, BUDDHIST, HINDU!

We all have a higher
Power we believe!

cherish Today

Do you know?

I AM...

A PERSON OF FAITH!

Cherish Today

Do you know?

FAITH, HOPE & LOVE!

THESE THREE!

BUT, THE GREATEST OF
THESE IS LOVE!

1.Corinthians 13:13

Cherish Today

Do you know?

FAITH, TRUST & GRATITUDE!

Give thanks to God
in Everything!

cherish Today

Do you know?

IN GOD WE TRUST!

Cherish Today

Do you know?

Love to you All!

May we stay in Prayer
For the greater good!

Cherish Today

Do you know?

ONCE YOU HAVE ALL THE FACTS

LET YOUR CONSCIENCE

BE YOUR GUIDE!

cherish Today

Do you know?

Practice Forgiveness...

It keeps our hearts true!

Cherish Today

Do you know?

A little kindness

goes a long way!

cherish Today

Do you know?

Thank you!

cherish Today

Do you know?

Dear God,
Forgive my unbelief!

Cherish Today

Do you know?

Some of us believe in
a Self-fulfilling Prophecy...

As you do...
Make your belief be about
the Power of Love!

cherish Today

Do you know?

Okay! So the Earth is
cleansing itself!

cherish Today

Do you know?

In the beginning God created
the heaven and the earth.

Genesis 1:1

cherish Today

Do you know?

WE ALL NEED HEALING!

FEED YOUR MIND, FEED YOUR

BODY, FEED YOUR SPIRIT!

NUTRITION IS KEY!

Cherish Today

Do you know?

MAY WE ALL GET

THE REST & HEALING TIME

WE NEED!

cherish Today

Do you know?

FEED YOUR SOUL!

Cherish Today

Do you know?

BIBLE, KORAN

TORAH (OLD TESTAMENT),

MEDITATION, YOGA,

PRAYER...

cherish Today

Do you know?

Prayers & Blessings go out
to all the health care professionals ...

May these angels be protected
by God, Himself!

cherish Today

Do you know?

SELF-CARE!

cherish Today

Do you know?

Census 2020 online,

My Broad Genealogy:

African-American (Nigerian),
German-Irish-French,
Sioux Indian (Blackfeet)
& Cherokee.

cherish Today

_____

_____

_____

_____

_____

_____

_____

_____

_____

_____

_____

_____

_____

_____

_____

_____

Do you know?
March 24,
Medicine is working for the
cure of COVID-19.
Thank you! God, for your Mercy! On us!

Praises to you my Lord & Savior!

cherish Today

Do you know?

Welcome! 21st Century...
Homeschooling!
Virtual classrooms at Home!

Cherish Today

Do you know?

Welcome! 21st Century...
Computers, Cell Phones,
Digital& Cable TV/Home Movies...
DVD, CD, DVR's, LP'S return

Cherish Today

Do you know?
Welcome 21st Century!

We've gone from the Flintstones
to the Jetsons in 2020 years!

cherish Today

Do you know?

ENTREPRENEURSHIP'S!

Individual Business Ownerships...
Home Office...
Working from Home!

cherish Today

Do you know?

SELF-EMPLOYMENT,

SELF-PUBLISHING...

SELF-OWNERSHIP!

SELF-ENTERPRISE!

cherish Today

Do you know?

Farms and Farmers!

They are our source for natural foods!

Cherish Today

Do you know?

Our natural resources
are essential to our survival!

cherish Today

Do you know?

My boss' grandmother
lived to be 119 years old...

She only ate what she grew from her yard!

cherish Today

Do you know?

Glad for canned foods, bottled juice,
washer machines & dryers...
all the modern conveniences!

cherish Today

Do you know?

Welcome! 21st Century...

Online shopping, online banking...
Credit/Debit cards!

cherish Today

Do you know?

Live in the Present Moment!

cherish Today

Do you know?

Grow Fruits & Vegetables
in your yard or neighborhood!

If you have fruit trees you are blessed!

cherish Today

Do you know?

Farmer's Markets & Tag Sales,

Flea Market Sales

we can do & depend on!

Cherish Today

_____

_____

_____

_____

_____

_____

_____

_____

_____

_____

_____

_____

_____

_____

_____

Do you know?

Brother, Brother... What's Going On?

-Marvin Gaye

cherish Today

Do you know?

Our Higher Power has prepared us for this!

May we keep our faith in the Lord!

cherish Today

Do you know?

Maybe I'm crazy...
with this fear I have of falling!

But, I believe in God's Good Plan!

Hoping for the best!

Cherish Today

Do you know?

May we all get through this!

Let's keep it together!

Love you guys!

cherish Today

Do you know?

WAIT ON THE LORD!

cherish Today

Do you know?

My Deepest Sympathy

to those who have lost a

Loved one during this time

of COVID-19.

Cherish Today

Do you know?

Catholic & Protestant Church Services
& Bible Study can be found everyday
of the week on TV & Radio!

cherish Today

Do you know?

Ministry of Dr. Charles F. Stanley,
T.D. Jakes, Reverend Dollar, 700 Club,
Shepherd's Chapel,
Super Soul Sunday &
EWTN Channel & Others.

cherish Today

Do you know?

One ounce of truth benefits
like ripples on a pond!

-Nikki Giovanni

cherish Today

Do you know?

Home Remedies:

Chicken Noodle Soup & Ginger Ale,

Tussin (cough syrups),

Tylenol, NyQuil, Vitamin C,

and
Apple Cider Vinegar
&
Garlic...

cherish Today

Do you know?

DRINK PLENTY OF FLUIDS!
Water, Fruit Juice & Soda!

Stay away from caffeine!

cherish Today

Do you know?

My favorite, most satisfying
& healthiest meal is
a fresh pot of homemade soup!

cherish Today

Do you know?

Learn to be still!

cherish Today

Do you know?

Spend Time in the Silence ...
Take the Time you need to Listen!

Cherish Today

Do you know?

Try K-Love Music!

cherish Today

_____
_____
_____
_____
_____
_____
_____
_____
_____
_____
_____
_____
_____
_____
_____
_____
_____

Do you know?

Patience is Virtue!

cherish Today

Do you know?

BE WELL!

About Covid-19 Review

My book of affirmations was created to inspire change in individuals & communities during these changing times.

What I've learned personally is that we can't go back... we can't change the past ...tomorrow's not promised, we can't predict the future... There are no guarantees! Be where you're at! We must stop trying to make it like it was...

Meet Him half-way and believe in what we have to offer each other: Being Loving and being in-love, Clean Sex vs Disease, Co-Creation with the Arts, Marriage and Family.

Nurture yourself with Mother Nature & be graced by Father Time.

Life is a gift...
Me, Myself... I'm Chasing Rainbows!

Peace!

www.ingramcontent.com/pod-product-compliance
Lightning Source LLC
Chambersburg PA
CBHW030653110726
47901CB00002B/700